# Things That Balance

Patty Whitehouse

Rourke
Publishing LLC
Vero Beach, Florida 32964

www.rourkepublishing.com

PHOTO CREDITS: © David and Patricia Armentrout: pages 4, 5, 6, 7, 10, 11, 14, 17, 18; © PIR: pages 13, 19; © Craig Lopetz: page 12; © constructionphotographs.com: pages 8, 9, 15, 16, 20; © Stefan Tordenmalm: page 21

Editor: Robert Stengard-Olliges

Cover and interior design by Nicola Stratford

**Library of Congress Cataloging-in-Publication Data**

Whitehouse, Patricia, 1958-
 Things that balance / Patty Whitehouse.
    p. cm. -- (Construction forces)
 Includes index.
 ISBN 1-60044-194-7 (hardcover)
 ISBN 1-59515-548-1 (softcover)
 1. Levers--Juvenile literature. 2. Mechanical movements--Juvenile literature. 3. Equilibrium--Juvenile literature. 4. Stability--Juvenile literature. 5. Building sites--Juvenile literature. I. Title. II. Series: Whitehouse, Patricia, 1958- Construction forces.
 TJ147.W4835 2007
 531'.3--dc22
                        2006008863

Printed in the USA

CG/CG

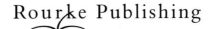

Rourke Publishing

www.rourkepublishing.com – sales@rourkepublishing.com
Post Office Box 3328, Vero Beach, FL 32964
1-800-394-7055

# Table of Contents

# Construction Site

This is a **construction site**. Workers build things here.

Some things at a construction site balance. Balanced things will not fall down.

# Things That Balance

Tools and **machines** need to balance. This truck needs help to balance.

Things that balance are **stable**. They do not fall over. That's useful at a construction site!

# Balance on Legs

A sawhorse balances on two legs. Two sawhorses hold wood for sawing.

The tripod balances on three legs. Workers use it to measure the land.

# Ladders Can Balance

Ladders help workers get up and down. Some ladders balance by leaning on a wall.

Some ladders have two sides. They can balance without leaning.

# Balance on Wire

A crane lifts a heavy **load**. The load has to balance for the crane to work.

A crane lifts heavy loads on a cable. The arm of the crane balances over the load.

# Scaffold Balance

Workers balance on a scaffold. The ropes help to keep the scaffold balanced.

This scaffold is on a scissor lift. It stays balanced as it moves up and down.

# People Balance

Some workers need good balance. So they do not fall down.

This roof is not **level**. The workers have to balance as they fix the roof.

# Up and Down Balance

A fork lift carries a load. The load balances on its lifting arms. Then the load goes up.

Harness

Some workers wear a harness when they work. They balance as they move up and down the building.

# Buildings and Balance

Workers measure when they build. Their buildings must be straight.

The Leaning **Tower** of Pisa is not balanced. It is not stable. Some day, it might fall over.

# Try It!

You can balance blocks to make a tower. How many can you balance?

# GLOSSARY

**construction site** (kuhn STRUHKT shun SITE): a place where workers build

**level** (LEV uhl): straight across

**load** (LOHD): something that is carried

**machine** (muh SEEN): something that uses energy to help people work

**stable** (STAY buhl): not easily moved

**tower** (TOU ur): a tall, thin building

# INDEX

## FURTHER READING

Gardner, Robert. *Heavy-duty Science Projects with Weight : How Much Does it Weigh?* Enslow Publishers, 2003.
Kilby, Don. *At a Construction Site.* Kids Can Press, 2003.
Rowe, Julian. *Keeping Your Balance*. Childrens Press, 1993.

## WEBSITES TO VISIT

http://science.howstuffworks.com/engineering-channel.htm
http://www.bobthebuilder.com/usa/index.html
http://www.sci.mus.mn.us/sln/tf/b/balance/balance.html

## ABOUT THE AUTHOR

Patty Whitehouse has been a teacher for 17 years. She is currently a Lead Science teacher in Chicago, where she lives with her husband and two teenage children. She is the author of more than 100 books about science for children.